KEIR STARMER

The Man Behind the Reform

Willie N. Foster

CONTENTS

Introduction

Keir Starmer has made a significant impact on British politics and law, marked by his journey from a determined young barrister to a key figure in the country's political landscape. Born on September 2, 1962, in Southwark, London, Keir grew up in a modest household, the son of a toolmaker and a nurse. His upbringing instilled in him a strong sense of justice and the importance of hard work.

Keir's journey into law began at the University of Leeds, followed by further studies at Oxford. As a barrister, he quickly made a name for himself by taking on challenging cases, often those that involved defending human rights. He fought for the underprivileged, those whose voices were often unheard, and stood up against injustices. His dedication and skill did not go unnoticed, and in 2008, he was appointed the Director of Public Prosecutions (DPP), a role that put him in charge of prosecuting criminal cases in England and Wales.

As DPP, Keir introduced several reforms aimed at making the legal system fairer and more transparent.

He worked tirelessly to improve the prosecution process for cases involving violence against women and hate crimes, ensuring that victims received the justice they deserved. His tenure was not without its challenges and controversies, but Keir's commitment to justice remained steadfast.

In 2015, Keir transitioned from law to politics, becoming the Member of Parliament for Holborn and St Pancras. This move was driven by his desire to make a broader impact on society. Within a short period, he rose through the ranks of the Labour Party, gaining respect for his principled stance on key issues, including Brexit. Keir's clear and thoughtful approach to complex problems set him apart, and in April 2020, he was elected Leader of the Labour Party.

As the leader, Keir faced the daunting task of uniting a divided party and presenting a viable alternative to the ruling government. He focused on rebuilding trust with the public, emphasising the need for integrity, transparency, and accountability in politics. His background in law informed his approach, bringing a meticulous and evidence-based perspective to political leadership.

Keir Starmer's impact on British politics and law is a testament to his unwavering commitment to justice and public service. He has continuously advocated for those who are often overlooked, striving to create a fairer society. His journey from a young lawyer fighting for human rights to the Leader of the Labour Party highlights the power of dedication and integrity in shaping a better future for all.

Chapter 1

Early Life and Family Background

Keir Starmer was born on September 2, 1962, in Southwark, London, into a family that was far from privileged but rich in values and strong work ethics. His father, Rodney Starmer, was a skilled toolmaker who worked tirelessly to support the family. He spent long hours crafting precision tools, a job that required both expertise and patience. Keir's mother, Josephine Baker, was a dedicated nurse. She had a lifelong battle with a debilitating illness called Still's disease, a severe form of arthritis that affected her mobility and health. Despite her condition, Josephine was a strong, loving presence in Keir's life.

Keir was the second of four children, and the Starmer household was always bustling with activity. Growing up in the small town of Oxted in Surrey, life was modest but filled with love and strong family bonds. The family did not have much money, but Rodney and Josephine instilled in their children the values of hard work, resilience, and the importance of helping others.

From a young age, Keir was known for his inquisitive nature and a keen sense of justice. He attended Reigate Grammar School, where he excelled academically. Even as a student, he was driven by a strong sense of fairness and was always ready to stand up for his classmates. His teachers remember him as a bright and dedicated student who was destined for great things.

Keir's interest in law and justice was apparent even during his school years. He was particularly influenced by his parents' commitment to helping others; his father's dedication to his craft and his mother's unwavering spirit despite her illness. These experiences shaped Keir's worldview and ignited a passion for fighting against injustice.

After finishing school, Keir went on to study law at the University of Leeds. This was a significant step, as he was the first in his family to attend university. His parents were immensely proud, and Keir was determined to make the most of this opportunity. At Leeds, he continued to excel, immersing himself in his studies and developing a deep understanding of the law.

Following his time at Leeds, Keir pursued further studies at St Edmund Hall, Oxford. Here, he not only honed his legal skills but also became involved in various social justice causes. He joined the Labour Party as a young student, driven by a desire to create a fairer society. His time at Oxford was pivotal, as it cemented his commitment to using the law as a tool for social change.

Keir's early life was marked by the values his parents instilled in him; hard work, fairness, and a commitment to helping others. His father's dedication to his work and his mother's resilience in the face of illness provided him with a strong foundation. These experiences were crucial in shaping his character and future career.

Despite the challenges, the Starmer family was close-knit and supportive. Keir often speaks about his parents with great admiration, crediting them for the values that guided him throughout his life. His father's meticulous nature and his mother's strength were key influences that inspired Keir to pursue a career where he could make a real difference.

Keir Starmer's early life and family background played a significant role in shaping the person he became. Growing up in a modest but loving home, he learned the importance of hard work, resilience, and standing up for what is right. These values guided him through his education and into his career in law and politics. The foundation laid by his parents' dedication and spirit set the stage for Keir's journey to becoming a prominent figure in British law and politics, driven by a relentless pursuit of justice and fairness.

1.1 Early Influences and Inspirations

Keir Starmer's journey to becoming a leading figure in British politics was profoundly shaped by early influences and inspirations. His background, education, and the people he encountered along the way played crucial roles in moulding his character and ambitions.

Growing up in Oxted, Surrey, Keir was deeply influenced by his parents. His father, Rodney Starmer, was a dedicated toolmaker who worked long hours to provide for the family.

Rodney's work ethic and meticulous nature left a lasting impression on Keir. Despite the physical demands of his job, Rodney always demonstrated a commitment to excellence and precision. Keir learned the value of hard work and dedication from watching his father.

Keir's mother, Josephine Baker, was another significant influence. As a nurse, she was devoted to helping others, even as she battled Still's disease, a severe form of arthritis. Her resilience and compassion deeply affected Keir. Josephine's determination to remain strong despite her illness inspired Keir to pursue a path where he could make a difference in people's lives. Her ability to care for others, even while facing her own struggles, instilled in him a profound sense of empathy and justice.

During his school years at Reigate Grammar School, Keir's sense of fairness and justice became evident. He was an excellent student, known for his dedication and intelligence. His teachers recognized his potential early on, noting his strong sense of right and wrong. Keir was not just focused on his studies; he was also keen on standing up for his classmates and ensuring everyone was treated fairly. This trait earned him respect among his peers and teachers.

After finishing school, Keir's educational journey took him to the University of Leeds, where he studied law. This was a pivotal moment in his life. Being the first in his family to attend university, Keir felt a deep responsibility to excel. At Leeds, he immersed himself in legal studies, developing a keen understanding of the law's potential to bring about social change. His professors at Leeds were instrumental in shaping his legal mind, encouraging him to think critically and advocate for justice.

Following his time at Leeds, Keir went on to further his studies at St Edmund Hall, Oxford. Here, he continued to hone his legal skills and became involved in various social justice causes. Oxford was a place where Keir's commitment to justice deepened. He was influenced by the academic environment, which encouraged rigorous debate and critical thinking. Additionally, his involvement in the Labour Party as a young student was driven by a desire to address social inequalities and fight for a fairer society.

During his time at Oxford, Keir was inspired by several mentors and figures in the field of law and politics. He looked up to prominent human rights lawyers and political leaders who used their positions to advocate for the marginalised and oppressed. These figures reinforced Keir's belief in the power of law as a tool for social justice.

Keir Starmer's early influences and inspirations were rooted in his family, education, and the people he met along the way. His parents' dedication and resilience provided a strong foundation, while his educational experiences at Leeds and Oxford shaped his legal mind and commitment to justice. The values instilled in him during these formative years guided his path towards becoming a prominent advocate for fairness and equality in both law and politics. Keir's journey is a testament to the impact of early influences and the enduring power of education in shaping one's aspirations and achievements.

Chapter 2

The Making of a Barrister

Keir Starmer's journey to becoming a barrister was driven by his deep sense of justice and dedication to helping others. After excelling at university, he entered the legal profession, quickly gaining a reputation for his hard work and commitment to human rights. This chapter explores Keir's early legal career, highlighting the key cases he worked on and the challenges he faced. His passion for defending the vulnerable and fighting against injustice set the stage for his impactful career in law and beyond.

2.1 Entry into the Legal Profession

Keir Starmer started his legal career with a strong passion for justice and fairness. After finishing his studies at the University of Leeds and St Edmund Hall, Oxford, he began working as a barrister in 1987. He joined Middle Temple, one of the Inns of Court in London. From the beginning, Keir was committed to using his legal skills to help people and make a positive impact on society.

He started working at Doughty Street Chambers, a place known for its focus on human rights law. Here, Keir found the perfect environment to match his values and ambitions. The chambers took on cases defending the rights of the underprivileged and those often ignored by society. This setting allowed Keir to work on cases that deeply resonated with his sense of justice and fairness.

One of the early and important cases in Keir's career was the McLibel case in the early 1990s. This case involved two environmental activists, Helen Steel and David Morris, who were sued by McDonald's for distributing leaflets criticising the company. The trial became one of the longest in English legal history. Keir was part of the defence team, working hard to protect the activists' right to free speech. This case was a significant milestone for Keir, showing his dedication to defending basic rights.

Another crucial case was Keir's work on the appeals of the Birmingham Six. This group of Irish men had been wrongly convicted of bombing two pubs in Birmingham in 1974. The case was a clear example of a miscarriage of justice, and Keir played a key role in overturning their convictions. This work highlighted Keir's commitment to correcting legal wrongs and ensuring justice.

In 2001, Keir reached a major milestone when he was made Queen's

Counsel (QC), a title given to top barristers in the UK. This recognition marked him as one of the leading lawyers in the country. Becoming a QC was not just a personal achievement; it also enabled Keir to take on more significant cases.

One notable case he worked on as QC was challenging the UK's involvement in the Iraq War. Keir partnered with human rights groups to argue that the war was illegal under international law. These cases were complex and politically sensitive, but Keir always focused on justice and the rule of law.

Besides his work in court, Keir also contributed to legal reforms. He helped draft guidelines and reports on human rights issues, influencing the development of human rights law in the UK. His work on the Human Rights Act was particularly significant, aiming to align UK laws with the European Convention on Human Rights.

In 2008, Keir's career took a new turn when he became the Director of Public Prosecutions (DPP) and head of the Crown Prosecution Service (CPS). In this role, he oversaw all criminal prosecutions in England and Wales. This position allowed him to make a broader impact on the criminal justice system. He introduced reforms to improve the prosecution process, especially in cases involving violence against women and hate crimes. Keir's time as DPP was marked by his dedication to fairness, transparency, and justice.

Throughout his career, Keir's main goal was to make a positive impact on society. His involvement in high-profile cases and contributions to legal reforms showed his unwavering commitment to justice. Keir's journey from a young barrister to a leading figure in the legal field was filled with significant milestones and key cases that demonstrated his dedication to defending the rights of the underprivileged and ensuring justice was served.

Keir Starmer's entry into the legal profession and his career were driven by a strong commitment to justice and human rights. From his early days at Doughty Street Chambers to his role as Director of Public Prosecutions, Keir consistently worked on cases and reforms aimed at protecting the vulnerable and upholding justice. His key cases and legal milestones reflect his dedication to making a meaningful difference in the legal field and society as a whole.

2.2 Human Rights Advocacy

Keir Starmer's commitment to human rights advocacy has been a cornerstone of his career. Throughout his journey as a barrister and later as a prominent figure in British politics, Keir has consistently fought to protect and promote human rights for all.

As a barrister at Doughty Street Chambers, Keir specialised in human rights law. He took on cases that involved defending the rights of marginalised groups, including victims of discrimination and injustice. His work often focused on challenging unfair treatment and advocating for equality under the law. Keir believed deeply in the principle that every person deserves to be treated with dignity and respect, regardless of their background or circumstances.

One of the landmark cases that highlighted Keir's dedication to human rights was his involvement in the McLibel case. This case centred around two activists who were sued by McDonald's for distributing leaflets criticising the company's practices. Keir was part of the legal team that defended the activists, arguing passionately for their right to freedom of expression. The case not only tested the limits of free speech but also underscored Keir's belief in defending individuals against powerful interests.

Keir's advocacy extended beyond the courtroom. He played a pivotal role in drafting and promoting human rights legislation, including the Human Rights Act. This legislation incorporated the European Convention on Human Rights into UK law, ensuring that individuals could seek redress for human rights violations in domestic courts. Keir's efforts to strengthen legal protections for human rights reflected his commitment to building a fairer and more just society.

In 2008, Keir's commitment to human rights was further demonstrated when he was appointed Director of Public Prosecutions (DPP). In this role, he oversaw the prosecution of criminal cases in England and Wales, including those involving human rights abuses. Keir introduced reforms aimed at improving how the criminal justice system handled cases of violence against women, hate crimes, and other forms of discrimination. His goal was to ensure that victims receive justice and that perpetrators were held accountable under the law.

Since entering politics and becoming the Leader of the Labour Party, Keir has continued to champion human rights as a fundamental pillar of his agenda. He has advocated for policies that protect civil liberties, uphold the rule of law, and promote equality for all individuals. Keir's leadership has emphasised the importance of respecting human rights both at home and abroad, ensuring that Britain remains committed to its obligations under international law.

Keir Starmer's advocacy for human rights has been characterised by a steadfast commitment to fairness, equality, and justice. From his early days as a barrister to his current role as a political leader, Keir has consistently fought to defend the rights of individuals and communities facing discrimination and injustice. His efforts have left a lasting impact on the legal and political landscape, shaping policies and laws that protect human rights and promote a more inclusive society for all.

Chapter 3

Director of Public Prosecutions

As Director of Public Prosecutions (DPP), Keir Starmer oversaw criminal prosecutions in England and Wales. Appointed in 2008, his role was to ensure that criminal cases were handled fairly and effectively. Keir introduced reforms to improve how the legal system dealt with cases involving violence against women, hate crimes, and other injustices. His tenure focused on upholding the rule of law and ensuring justice for victims while maintaining transparency and accountability in prosecutions.

3.1   Appointment and Responsibilities as Director of Public Prosecutions

Keir Starmer's role as Director of Public Prosecutions (DPP) began in 2008 and was a major step in his legal career. As the leader of the Crown Prosecution Service (CPS), he was in charge of all criminal prosecutions in England and Wales. This job was vital for making sure the criminal justice system was fair and worked well.

One of Keir's main duties as DPP was to ensure the rule of law was upheld. This meant that everyone, no matter who they were, should be treated fairly by the legal system. Keir strongly believed that justice should be available to everyone and that the legal system should protect victims' rights while ensuring fair trials for those accused of crimes.

During his time as DPP, Keir introduced many reforms to improve how the CPS handled cases. He focused on bettering the prosecution of crimes such as violence against women and hate crimes, which needed special attention and expertise. Keir aimed to make it easier to bring criminals to justice and to provide better support for victims during the legal process.

Another key part of Keir's job was to lead and guide prosecutors across England and Wales. He ensured that prosecutors did their jobs with honesty and professionalism. Keir emphasised the need for transparency and accountability within the CPS, wanting to build trust between the public and the criminal justice system.

Keir's time as DPP came with its own set of challenges. He dealt with complex cases and tough decisions that required balancing legal rules with practical realities. Some cases were highly publicised and brought intense scrutiny, but Keir remained committed to maintaining high standards in legal practice.

Throughout his role, Keir was dedicated to making the criminal justice system more effective and fair. He worked with police, victim support groups, and legal professionals to address problems and implement changes. Keir's approach was always driven by his belief that the legal system should serve justice and the public interest.

Keir Starmer's appointment as Director of Public Prosecutions was a key point in his career. He took on the responsibility of managing criminal prosecutions with a strong commitment to fairness, justice, and the rule of law. Keir's time as DPP was marked by efforts to improve the prosecution process and support victims while upholding the integrity of the legal system. His leadership had a lasting impact on the CPS and helped shape discussions about the role of prosecutors in ensuring justice in society.

3.2 Major Prosecutions, Reforms, Challenges and Controversies

Keir Starmer's time as Director of Public Prosecutions (DPP) was filled with significant prosecutions, meaningful reforms, and various challenges and controversies. His role at the Crown Prosecution Service (CPS) showed his strong dedication to justice and his willingness to tackle tough issues.

One of the major prosecutions during Keir's tenure was the case against Levi Bellfield, a serial killer responsible for the murders of several young women. This case was extremely complex and required meticulous work. Keir's leadership ensured that Bellfield was brought to justice, highlighting his commitment to prosecuting dangerous criminals and protecting the public.

Keir also oversaw the prosecution of the killers of Rachel Nickell. Rachel was tragically murdered in 1992, and for years, her case remained unsolved. Through determined efforts and new forensic techniques, the CPS was able to bring her killer to justice under Keir's leadership. This prosecution brought closure to Rachel's family and demonstrated Keir's dedication to solving even the most challenging cases.

Another significant case was the prosecution of the killers of Damilola Taylor, a young boy who was murdered in London in 2000. Damilola's death shocked the nation, and bringing his killers to justice was a top priority. Keir's work on this case showcased his commitment to seeking justice for victims and their families, no matter how difficult the case might be.

Keir was also very focused on implementing reforms to improve the CPS and the wider criminal justice system. One of his main areas of focus was addressing issues related to violence against women and hate crimes.

He introduced new guidelines for prosecuting cases of domestic violence. Keir recognized that these cases needed a careful and informed approach, so he aimed to make sure that victims were better supported and that prosecution rates improved. His reforms included measures to make the process less daunting for victims and to ensure they received the justice they deserved.

Keir also worked on improving the prosecution of hate crimes. He introduced new policies to make sure these crimes were identified and prosecuted more effectively. His efforts aimed to show that hate crimes would not be tolerated and that the legal system would act strongly against those who committed such offences.

Transparency and accountability within the CPS were also important to Keir. He made efforts to ensure that decisions made by prosecutors were clear and that the public could trust the justice system. This included publishing more information about how prosecution decisions were made and being more open with the public and the media.

Keir's time as DPP wasn't without its challenges and controversies. One major controversy was the decision not to prosecute the police officers involved in the death of Ian Tomlinson during the 2009 G20 protests. Tomlinson, a newspaper vendor, died after being struck by a police officer. The decision not to prosecute caused public outrage and raised questions about police accountability and the CPS's decision-making process.

Handling historical sexual abuse cases was another challenge. While Keir was praised for taking these cases seriously and working to bring perpetrators to justice, there were criticisms about how long it took to prosecute some cases and the perceived inconsistencies in handling different cases. These challenges showed the difficulties in prosecuting complex and sensitive historical cases.

Keir also faced criticism over cases involving deaths in police custody. These cases were highly sensitive and often emotionally charged, making decisions about prosecution particularly difficult. Despite his commitment to handling these cases fairly and transparently, the criticisms highlighted the ongoing challenges faced by the CPS in dealing with such complex situations.

Keir Starmer's time as Director of Public Prosecutions was marked by significant prosecutions, important reforms, and various challenges and controversies. His leadership at the

CPS showed his strong commitment to justice, fairness, and transparency. Through his efforts to prosecute high-profile cases like those of Levi Bellfield, the killers of Rachel Nickell, and Damilola Taylor, as well as his reforms to improve the justice system, Keir left a lasting impact. His work highlighted his dedication to protecting the rights of individuals, holding powerful figures accountable, and ensuring that the legal system operated fairly and effectively.

Chapter 4

Transition to Politics

Keir Starmer's move from the legal world to politics marked a significant change in his career. After years of ensuring justice as Director of Public Prosecutions, Keir felt the need to make a broader impact. He decided to enter politics to help shape laws and policies that would create a fairer society. This chapter explores Keir's reasons for making this shift, his early political journey, and the principles that guided him as he transitioned from a legal expert to a political leader.

4.1 Decision to Enter Politics and Election as MP for Holborn and St Pancras

Keir Starmer's decision to transition from a distinguished legal career to the political arena was driven by a desire to make broader societal changes. After serving as Director of Public Prosecutions (DPP), where he had made significant strides in upholding justice, Keir felt that the next step was to influence the creation and implementation of laws at the highest level. He believed that by entering politics, he could help shape policies that would benefit society as a whole.

Keir's motivation to enter politics was deeply rooted in his personal values and experiences. Throughout his career, he had witnessed firsthand the impact of legislation on people's lives, both positively and negatively. His work in the legal field, particularly in human rights and public prosecutions, made him acutely aware of the gaps in the system and the areas that required reform. He saw politics as a way to address these issues more effectively and to advocate for the rights and needs of ordinary people.

In 2014, Keir announced his decision to stand for Parliament as a Labour Party candidate. He chose to run for the seat of Holborn and St Pancras, a constituency with a rich history and diverse population. This area of London resonated with Keir due to its vibrant community and the social issues it faced, which aligned with his commitment to justice and equality.

Keir's campaign for the 2015 general election was driven by his vision for a fairer society. He focused on key issues such as affordable housing, access to quality education, and healthcare for all. His legal background gave him a unique perspective on these issues, and he promised to bring his experience and dedication to Parliament to fight for the constituents of Holborn and St Pancras.

Keir's approach to campaigning was very much grounded in his personal principles. He engaged with local residents, listened to their concerns, and discussed his plans to address the challenges they faced. His ability to connect with people and his genuine commitment to making a difference earned him widespread support.

One of the key moments in Keir's campaign was his emphasis on social justice. He spoke passionately about the need for a government that would work for everyone, not just the privileged few. He highlighted his work as a barrister and as DPP, demonstrating his long-standing commitment to fighting for justice and equality. This resonated with many voters who were looking for a representative who genuinely understood their struggles and was committed to addressing them.

In May 2015, Keir Starmer was elected as the Member of Parliament (MP) for Holborn and St Pancras. Winning this seat was a significant achievement and a testament to his hard work and dedication during the campaign. It also marked the beginning of a new chapter in his career, one where he could directly influence the legislative process and work towards the reforms he believed were necessary.

As an MP, Keir continued to focus on the issues that mattered most to his constituents. He was a strong advocate for social justice, human rights, and equality. His speeches in Parliament and his work in committees reflected his deep understanding of the law and his commitment to using that knowledge to benefit society. He quickly established himself as a diligent and effective representative, gaining respect from colleagues across the political spectrum.

Keir's election as an MP also set the stage for his future roles within the Labour Party. His dedication and capability did not go unnoticed, and he was soon given important responsibilities within the party. His experience as a barrister and his tenure as DPP provided him with the skills needed to navigate the complexities of political life and to advocate effectively for his policies and ideals.

Keir Starmer's decision to enter politics was driven by a desire to create meaningful change and to address the injustices he had seen throughout his legal career. His election as MP for Holborn and St Pancras was a result of his commitment to justice, his ability to connect with voters, and his unwavering dedication to the principles of fairness and equality. As an MP, Keir continued to advocate for the rights of his constituents and to push for reforms that would benefit society as a whole, marking the beginning of a significant political career.

4.2   Initial   Parliamentary Contributions

After being elected as the Member of Parliament (MP) for Holborn and St Pancras in 2015, Keir Starmer quickly began to make his mark in Parliament. His background as a lawyer and former Director of Public Prosecutions gave him a unique perspective and set of skills that he brought to his new role.

One of Keir's first priorities was to address the issues that mattered most to his constituents. He was deeply committed to social justice, and this was evident in his initial parliamentary contributions. He spoke passionately about the need for affordable housing, quality education, and accessible healthcare. These were not just political talking points for Keir; they were issues he genuinely cared about and had seen the impact of in his previous work.

Keir's legal expertise also came into play as he took on complex issues in Parliament. He quickly became known for his thoughtful and well-researched contributions to debates. He used his knowledge to scrutinise government policies and legislation, always with an eye towards how they would affect ordinary people. Keir was particularly focused on ensuring that laws were fair and just, and he was not afraid to challenge proposals that he believed would lead to inequality or injustice.

One of the key areas where Keir made significant contributions was in human rights. Given his extensive background in this field, he was well-equipped to speak on matters related to civil liberties and justice. He advocated strongly for the protection of human rights both within the UK and internationally. Keir was a vocal critic of any measures that he felt would undermine individual freedoms or erode the rule of law.

Keir also played an active role in various parliamentary committees. These committees are essential for examining specific issues in detail and holding the government to account. Keir's participation in these committees allowed him to use his analytical skills to contribute to important inquiries and reports. His work in committees further established his reputation as a diligent and knowledgeable MP who was committed to thorough scrutiny and evidence-based decision-making.

Another significant aspect of Keir's initial contributions was his engagement with his constituents. He understood the importance of staying connected to the people he represented. Keir regularly held surgeries and meetings to listen to their concerns and to ensure that their voices were heard in Parliament. He was dedicated to being a responsive and effective representative, always aiming to address the issues that were most important to his community.

Keir's early years in Parliament also saw him taking a stand on issues such as Brexit. He was deeply involved in the debates and discussions surrounding the UK's decision to leave the European Union. Keir argued for a Brexit deal that would protect jobs, workers' rights, and the economy. His contributions were informed by his commitment to ensuring that the process was conducted fairly and transparently, with the best interests of the public in mind.

Keir Starmer's initial parliamentary contributions were marked by his dedication to justice, his legal expertise, and his commitment to his constituents. He quickly established himself as a thoughtful and principled MP who was willing to tackle complex issues and stand up for what he believed in. Keir's early work in Parliament laid the foundation for his future roles and responsibilities, as he continued to advocate for fairness, equality, and the protection of human rights.

Chapter 5

Rise within the Labour Party

Keir Starmer's rise within the Labour Party was swift and remarkable. After becoming an MP, his dedication, legal expertise, and passion for social justice quickly earned him respect and recognition. He took on key roles, showcasing his ability to lead and make impactful decisions. This chapter explores Keir's journey through the ranks of the Labour Party, his influential positions, and how he became a prominent figure, shaping the party's direction and policies. His commitment to fairness and equality continued to guide his political career.

5.1 Roles within the Labour Party and Brexit Stance and Influence

After being elected as the MP for Holborn and St Pancras in 2015, Keir Starmer quickly began to rise within the Labour Party. His background as a lawyer and former Director of Public Prosecutions, coupled with his passion for social justice, helped him earn the respect and trust of his colleagues. As he took on various roles within the party, he became known for his thoughtful approach, dedication, and leadership skills.

Keir's first significant role within the Labour Party was when he was appointed Shadow Minister for Immigration in September 2015. In this position, he was responsible for scrutinising the government's immigration policies and offering alternative solutions. Keir approached this role with his characteristic thoroughness, focusing on fairness and justice in the immigration system. He emphasised the need for compassionate and humane treatment of immigrants while ensuring that the system was robust and effective.

In October 2016, Keir was promoted to Shadow Secretary of State for Exiting the European Union, a critical role given the political landscape at the time. This position put Keir at the forefront of one of the most significant issues facing the UK; Brexit. As Shadow Brexit Secretary,

Keir was responsible for shaping Labour's stance on Brexit and holding the government accountable for its handling of the process. His legal expertise and meticulous nature made him well-suited for this challenging role.

Brexit was one of the most contentious and complex issues in British politics during Keir's early years in Parliament. The decision to leave the European Union (EU) had divided the country, and there were numerous debates about how to proceed. Keir played a crucial role in shaping Labour's approach to Brexit, advocating for a balanced and pragmatic stance.

Keir believed that while the UK had voted to leave the EU, it was essential to ensure that the process was handled in a way that protected jobs, workers' rights, and the economy. He argued for a Brexit deal that would maintain a close relationship with the EU, emphasising the importance of trade, security, and cooperation. Keir's position was driven by his commitment to protecting the interests of ordinary people and minimising the potential negative impacts of Brexit.

One of Keir's key contributions was his insistence on the need for a meaningful vote in Parliament on the final Brexit deal. He argued that MPs should have the opportunity to scrutinise and approve any deal negotiated by the government. This stance was rooted in his belief in parliamentary sovereignty and democratic accountability. Keir's efforts were instrumental in ensuring that Parliament had a say in the Brexit process, which was a significant achievement.

Keir also advocated for a customs union with the EU, which would allow for tariff-free trade and help prevent a hard border between Northern Ireland and the Republic of Ireland. He was deeply concerned about the potential impact of Brexit on peace and stability in Northern Ireland, and he worked tirelessly to ensure that this issue was given the attention it deserved.

Throughout the Brexit negotiations, Keir remained a vocal advocate for protecting workers' rights, environmental standards, and consumer protections. He was determined to ensure that these important safeguards were not compromised as the UK left the EU.

Keir's approach to Brexit was characterised by his commitment to evidence-based decision-making, transparency, and accountability.

Keir's influence on Labour's Brexit stance was significant. He played a key role in shaping the party's policy and strategy, often leading debates and discussions within the party. His thoughtful and principled approach helped to steer Labour towards a position that balanced respecting the referendum result with protecting the country's interests.

Keir's work on Brexit also earned him recognition beyond the Labour Party. He became known as one of the most knowledgeable and effective voices on Brexit in Parliament. His legal background, attention to detail, and commitment to fairness made him a respected figure in the debates and discussions surrounding Brexit.

Keir Starmer's roles within the Labour Party and his stance on Brexit were marked by his dedication to justice, fairness, and the protection of ordinary people's interests. As Shadow Minister for Immigration and later as Shadow Brexit Secretary, Keir demonstrated his ability to lead, influence, and navigate complex political issues. His approach to Brexit, characterised by pragmatism and a commitment to protecting key rights and standards, showcased his principled and thoughtful leadership. Through his work, Keir helped shape Labour's policies and played a significant role in one of the most important political issues of his time.

5.2 Leadership Campaign and Victory

Keir Starmer's path to becoming the leader of the Labour Party is a tale of hard work, dedication, and strong principles. After his role as the Shadow Brexit Secretary and his prominent part in the Brexit debates, Keir decided to run for the Labour Party leadership in 2020.

Deciding to run for leadership was a significant choice for Keir. The Labour Party was struggling after a heavy loss in the 2019 general election. Many members felt the party needed new direction and a leader who could bring everyone together. Keir believed he had the vision and experience to guide the party through tough times and regain the trust of voters.

Keir's campaign was centred on unity, competence, and returning to Labour's core values. He promised to focus on social justice, equality, and ensuring everyone had a fair chance, no matter their background. His legal career and human rights work appealed to many party members who wanted a leader with a strong moral foundation and proven dedication to justice.

During the campaign, Keir stressed the importance of listening to and learning from the party's traditional supporters, especially working-class communities who felt overlooked. He travelled around the country, meeting with party members and the public to hear their concerns and share his ideas for the future. His ability to connect with people and his genuine interest in their lives helped him gain significant support.

Keir also highlighted the need for Labour to be a strong and credible opposition to the Conservative government. He argued that the party needed to be united and effective in holding the government accountable and presenting a compelling alternative. His campaign emphasised practical solutions to the country's problems, like the housing crisis, underfunded public services, and inequality.

Keir's campaign received important endorsements from different parts of the Labour Party, including trade unions, MPs, and grassroots members. These endorsements were vital in building momentum and showing that Keir had broad support across the party. His calm, steady approach and clear vision appealed to many who wanted stability and reliable leadership.

The leadership election happened as the COVID-19 pandemic was unfolding, adding extra challenges. Despite these difficulties, Keir's campaign continued to gain support. When the results were announced in April 2020, Keir won decisively, getting 56.2% of the vote in the first round. This strong victory showed widespread support for his vision and ability to unite the party.

After winning, Keir pledged to work hard to earn the trust of the British people and rebuild the Labour Party. He emphasised the need for unity within the party and the importance of being a strong opposition. Keir also committed to tackling the immediate challenges of the pandemic and addressing long-term issues like economic inequality and climate change.

Keir's leadership campaign and victory marked a new beginning for the Labour Party. His focus on unity, competence, and social justice resonated with many members and supporters. As leader, Keir aimed to reconnect with the party's traditional base while appealing to a broader electorate.

Keir Starmer's leadership campaign was marked by his dedication to Labour's core values, his ability to connect with people, and his clear vision for the future. His decisive victory in the leadership election showed strong support for his approach and set the stage for his efforts to guide the Labour Party through tough times towards a fairer and more equitable society.

Chapter 6

Leadership of the Labour Party

Keir Starmer's leadership of the Labour Party marked a significant shift for the party. After winning the leadership election in 2020, he set out to rebuild trust with voters, unite the party, and tackle pressing issues like the COVID-19 pandemic. This chapter explores how Keir approached his role as leader, his efforts to address key challenges, and his vision for a fairer and more just society. Through his leadership, Keir aimed to revitalise the

Labour Party and position it as a strong alternative to the Conservative government.

6.1 Early Challenges and Strategies

When Keir Starmer became the Labour Party leader in April 2020, he faced many challenges. The party had suffered a big loss in the 2019 general election, and there was a lot of work needed to win back the voters' trust. On top of that, the COVID-19 pandemic was causing widespread problems and hardships. Keir knew he had to act quickly and effectively to tackle these issues.

One of Keir's first tasks was to rebuild trust with the public. Many people felt the Labour Party no longer represented their interests. Keir aimed to reconnect with these voters by listening to their concerns and showing that Labour was committed to addressing their needs. He stressed the importance of unity within the party, believing that a divided party could not effectively serve the public. Keir promised that Labour would be a responsible and credible opposition, holding the government accountable while also offering constructive solutions. His calm and steady approach was intended to show voters that Labour was serious about governing and making positive changes.

The COVID-19 pandemic was an immediate and pressing challenge. Keir had to manage the complexities of a public health crisis while establishing his leadership. He called for clear and consistent communication from the government and pushed for measures to protect public health and support those affected by the pandemic. Keir advocated for better support for frontline workers, increased testing and tracing, and more financial help for businesses and individuals struggling due to the pandemic. He also emphasised the importance of addressing the inequalities that the pandemic had worsened, such as its impact on low-income families and minority communities.

Keir understood that for Labour to be effective, the party needed to be united. He worked on bringing together different factions within the party and promoting a sense of common purpose. Keir focused on shared values and goals rather than internal disputes. He also initiated internal reforms to modernise the party and make it more efficient. This included improving communication within the party, updating its structures, and ensuring that the party's policies reflected the needs and concerns of its members and the public.

Setting a clear vision for the future was another key part of Keir's strategy. He aimed to present Labour as a party that could offer practical and achievable solutions to the country's problems. Keir focused on issues such as creating good jobs, building affordable housing, improving public services, and tackling climate change. He also emphasised the importance of fairness and social justice. Keir wanted to show that Labour was committed to creating a society where everyone had the opportunity to succeed, regardless of their background. This meant addressing issues like economic inequality, discrimination, and lack of access to quality education and healthcare.

Keir made it a priority to engage with the public and understand their concerns. He regularly visited communities across the country, listening to people's stories and discussing how Labour could help. This hands-on approach helped him connect with voters and demonstrate that he was genuinely interested in making their lives better. He also used various platforms, including social media, to communicate Labour's message and vision. By being accessible and responsive, Keir aimed to build a stronger relationship between the party and the public.

Keir Starmer's early days as Labour leader were marked by significant challenges, but he approached them with determination and a clear strategy. Rebuilding trust, addressing the pandemic, uniting the party, setting a clear vision, and engaging with the public were all crucial components of his approach. Through these efforts, Keir aimed to position Labour as a credible and effective alternative to the Conservative government, dedicated to creating a fairer and more just society for all.

6.2 Policy Positions and Reforms

Keir Starmer's leadership of the Labour Party has been defined by his clear policy positions and a strong focus on reforms. His approach is driven by a desire to address the major issues facing the UK and to create a fairer society for everyone.

One of Keir's key policy positions is on the economy. He believes in building an economy that works for all, not just the wealthy. This means focusing on creating good jobs, ensuring fair wages, and supporting small businesses. Keir has proposed raising the minimum wage to ensure that everyone earns a living wage. He also advocates for stronger workers' rights, including better job security and fair treatment in the workplace. By supporting small businesses, Keir aims to boost local economies and create opportunities in communities across the country.

Housing is another major focus for Keir. He recognizes that the UK faces a housing crisis, with many people unable to afford decent homes. Keir has called for a significant increase in the construction of affordable housing. He believes that everyone should have access to safe and affordable housing, and that the government should play a role in making this a reality. Keir's housing policy includes measures to tackle homelessness, support for renters, and reforms to make housing more affordable for first-time buyers.

Public services are at the heart of Keir's vision for a better society. He is committed to strengthening the National Health Service (NHS), ensuring that it is properly funded and can provide high-quality care for everyone. Keir has promised to address the staffing shortages in the NHS and to improve working conditions for healthcare workers. He also supports increased investment in education, aiming to give every child the best start in life. This includes reducing class sizes, improving school facilities, and ensuring that all children have access to a broad and balanced curriculum.

Climate change is another critical issue for Keir. He believes that urgent action is needed to tackle the climate crisis and to protect the environment for future generations. Keir has set out ambitious plans for a Green New Deal, which includes measures to reduce carbon emissions, promote renewable energy, and create green jobs. He supports investment in public transportation to reduce reliance on cars and to make it easier for people to travel sustainably. Keir's climate policy also includes protecting natural habitats and promoting biodiversity.

Social justice is a core principle for Keir. He is committed to tackling inequality and discrimination in all its forms. This includes addressing economic inequality, ensuring that everyone has access to the same opportunities, and promoting diversity and inclusion. Keir supports policies to reduce the gender pay gap, to ensure equal rights for LGBTQ+ people, and to tackle racial discrimination. He believes that a fair society is one where everyone is treated with dignity and respect, and where no one is left behind.

Keir's approach to reform is practical and focused on achieving real change. He believes in listening to people's concerns and working collaboratively to find solutions. This means engaging with communities, trade unions, businesses, and experts to develop policies that are effective and that address the real needs of the country. Keir's leadership style is based on integrity, transparency, and accountability. He is committed to making decisions that are in the best interests of the public and to building a government that is open and responsive.

Keir Starmer's policy positions and reforms are centred on creating a fairer, more just, and more sustainable society. His focus on the economy, housing, public services, climate change, and social justice reflects his commitment to addressing the key challenges facing the UK. Through his practical and principled approach, Keir aims to build a better future for everyone, ensuring that no one is left behind.

6.3 Handling Crises and Opposition

Handling crises and opposition have been central to Keir Starmer's leadership of the Labour Party. From the beginning, he has faced numerous challenges, but his calm and steady approach has helped him manage these tough situations.

One of the first major crises Keir dealt with was the COVID-19 pandemic. The pandemic caused huge disruptions in everyday life, impacting people's health, jobs, and overall well-being. Keir had to balance being a responsible opposition leader with offering constructive criticism to the government. He called for clear and consistent communication from the government, pushing for better support for frontline workers, more testing and tracing, and financial help for those struggling because of the pandemic. Keir focused on making sure the government's response was effective and fair, working to hold them accountable while also supporting measures that would help the public.

Another crisis Keir faced was within his own party. After a significant loss in the 2019 general election, the Labour Party was divided and needed direction. Keir made uniting the party a priority, bringing together different factions and promoting a sense of common purpose. He emphasised the importance of focusing on shared values and goals rather than internal disputes. By working to rebuild trust within the party and listening to the concerns of its members, Keir aimed to create a more cohesive and effective Labour Party.

In addition to handling these crises, Keir has also had to deal with opposition from the Conservative government. As leader of the opposition, his role is to hold the government accountable and offer alternative solutions to the country's problems. Keir has done this by focusing on key issues such as the economy, public services, and social justice. He has challenged the government's policies when he believes they are not in the public's best interest and has proposed practical and achievable alternatives.

For example, on economic issues, Keir has criticised the government's handling of the cost-of-living crisis, arguing that more needs to be done to support those struggling to make ends meet. He has proposed raising the minimum wage, providing better support for small businesses, and ensuring fair wages for all workers. Keir's focus is on creating an economy that benefits everyone, not just the wealthy.

On public services, Keir has emphasised the need for better funding and support for the National Health Service (NHS) and education. He has criticised cuts to these essential services and called for increased investment to ensure that everyone has access to high-quality healthcare and education. By focusing on these key issues, Keir aims to show that Labour can offer a credible and effective alternative to the Conservative government.

Throughout his leadership, Keir has also faced personal attacks and criticism from political opponents. He has handled these with dignity and composure, concentrating on the issues rather than getting drawn into negative or divisive rhetoric. Keir's approach is to stay true to his principles and focus on what is best for the country.

Keir Starmer's handling of crises and opposition has been marked by his calm and steady approach. He has navigated the challenges of the COVID-19 pandemic, worked to unite the Labour Party, and held the Conservative government accountable on key issues. Through his focus on practical solutions and his commitment to fairness and social justice, Keir aims to provide a credible and effective alternative to the current government, showing that Labour can lead the country through difficult times and towards a better future for all.

Chapter 7

Personal Life and Values

Keir Starmer's personal life and values have greatly influenced his leadership style and political decisions. This chapter explores his upbringing, family life, and the core values that shape his vision for a fairer society. Understanding Keir's background helps to see the person behind the politician, revealing how his personal experiences have driven his commitment to justice, equality, and public service. Through his personal story, we gain insight into what motivates him to fight for a better future for everyone.

7.1 Family and Personal Relationships

Keir Starmer's family and personal relationships have significantly shaped who he is. He grew up in a working-class family in Southwark, London. His father, Rodney, was a toolmaker, and his mother, Josephine, was a nurse. Keir often speaks about his parents with great respect and admiration, emphasising their strong work ethic and dedication. His mother, in particular, had a big impact on him. She suffered from a rare disease called Still's disease, which caused her a lot of pain and required constant medical care. Despite her illness, she remained resilient and caring, which deeply influenced Keir.

Keir's parents taught him the values of hard work, fairness, and helping others. These values have stayed with him throughout his life and are evident in his political career. Keir often shares stories about the struggles his parents faced and how their experiences shaped his views on social justice and equality. He believes that everyone, regardless of their background, should have the chance to succeed and live a dignified life.

Keir is married to Victoria Alexander, who works in occupational health. They have two children, a son and a daughter. Keir is known to be a devoted family man, often balancing his demanding career with spending quality time with his family. He speaks warmly of his wife and children, and it is clear they are central to his life. Victoria has been a supportive partner, standing by him through the ups and downs of his career in law and politics.

For Keir, family life means creating a stable and loving environment for his children. He wants them to grow up with the same values his parents taught him. Despite his busy schedule, Keir makes sure to be present in his children's lives, attending school events and spending time with them at home. He believes being a good parent means being there for your children and supporting them in their pursuits.

Keir also maintains strong relationships with his siblings. He has three sisters, and they have all stayed close over the years. The Starmer family is tight-knit, often coming together to support each other. This sense of family unity is something Keir values deeply and tries to foster in his own home.

Keir's personal relationships extend beyond his family. He has a close circle of friends and colleagues who have supported him throughout his career. These relationships have been crucial in providing him with advice, encouragement, and a sense of community. Keir values loyalty and trust in his friendships, and he is known for being a reliable and caring friend.

Keir Starmer's family and personal relationships have been a cornerstone of his life. They have shaped his values, influenced his career choices, and provided him with the support needed to navigate the challenges of his professional life. His upbringing in a hardworking family, his role as a husband and father, and his close relationships with friends and colleagues all contribute to the person he is today. Keir's commitment to his family and his strong personal values are evident in his approach to politics, where he strives to create a fairer and more just society for everyone.

7.2 Hobbies and interests

Keir Starmer, despite his busy political career, has hobbies and interests that provide balance and relaxation in his life. These personal pursuits offer a glimpse into his character beyond his professional responsibilities.

One of Keir's well known hobbies is playing football. He has been a passionate football fan since childhood and enjoys both watching and playing the sport. He supports Arsenal Football Club, and attending matches or watching games on television is a favourite pastime.

Playing football allows him to stay active and fit, while also providing an opportunity to unwind and have fun. It's a way for him to connect with friends and family, sharing the excitement and camaraderie that the sport brings.

Another interest of Keir's is music. He has a deep appreciation for various genres and enjoys listening to music in his free time. Keir's taste in music is diverse, ranging from classical to contemporary. Music provides him with a sense of relaxation and helps him unwind after a long day. It also serves as a source of inspiration and reflection, allowing him to take a break from the demands of his political life and recharge.

Reading is also one of Keir's favourite hobbies. He enjoys reading books on a wide range of topics, including history, politics, and fiction. Reading allows him to gain new perspectives and insights, which can be valuable in his role as a political leader. It also offers a way to escape into different worlds and stories, providing a mental break from his daily responsibilities. Keir believes that reading is essential for personal growth and lifelong learning, and he often encourages others to develop a love for books.

Keir also enjoys spending time outdoors, especially hiking and walking. He finds that being in nature helps him relax and clear his mind. Whether it's a simple walk in the park or a hike in the countryside, these outdoor activities provide a much-needed break from the hustle and bustle of city life. They also offer a chance to connect with nature and appreciate the beauty of the natural world.

In addition to these hobbies, Keir values quality time with his family. He enjoys simple activities like cooking and eating meals together, playing board games, or just having a chat. Family time is precious to him, and he makes an effort to prioritise it despite his busy schedule. These moments of togetherness strengthen his bond with his loved ones and provide a sense of balance and support in his life.

Keir Starmer's hobbies and interests reveal a well-rounded individual who values balance and relaxation. Whether it's playing football, enjoying music, reading, spending time outdoors, or being with family, these activities help him recharge and maintain a healthy work-life balance. They also provide a deeper understanding of the person behind the politician, showing his appreciation for simple pleasures and the importance of personal well-being.

7.3 Core Values and Principles

Keir Starmer's core values and principles are the foundation of his actions and decisions, both personally and politically. These beliefs, shaped by his upbringing and experiences, influence his vision for a better society.

Fairness is at the heart of Keir's beliefs. He believes everyone should have an equal opportunity in life, regardless of where they come from. This means creating chances for everyone to succeed, ensuring that no one is left behind. His commitment to fairness is clear in his policies aimed at reducing inequality, improving access to education, and supporting workers' rights. Keir's sense of fairness stems from his own childhood in a working-class family, where he saw firsthand the challenges people face and the importance of giving everyone a fair chance.

Justice is another core principle for Keir. As a former lawyer and Director of Public Prosecutions, he has dedicated much of his career to fighting for justice. He believes in the importance of the law being applied equally to all, and he works to reform the legal system and protect human rights. Keir's dedication to justice is driven by his belief in fairness and equality for all.

Compassion is also central to Keir's values. He understands the importance of kindness and empathy in bringing about positive change. This compassion drives his efforts to tackle issues like homelessness, poverty, and healthcare. Keir believes that a society should be judged by how it treats its most vulnerable members, and he works to create policies that offer support and respect to those in need. His compassionate approach is rooted in his upbringing, where he learned the importance of caring for others and standing up for what is right.

Integrity is another key value for Keir. He believes in being honest and transparent in his leadership. Keir is committed to serving the public interest and upholding high ethical standards. His integrity guides his actions, ensuring he remains focused on what is best for the people. Keir's integrity is evident in his straightforward communication and willingness to admit mistakes and learn from them. He understands that trust is essential in leadership and works hard to earn and maintain the trust of the public.

Keir also values collaboration and teamwork. He believes that working together with others is vital for achieving lasting change. This principle is reflected in his efforts to unite the Labour Party and build consensus on important issues. Keir recognizes that diverse perspectives and collective effort lead to better solutions. He is committed to listening to different viewpoints and working collaboratively to address the country's challenges.

Keir Starmer's core values like fairness, justice, compassion, integrity, and collaboration shape his approach to leadership and his vision for a fairer and more just society. These values, shaped by his life experiences, guide his policies and actions, driving his commitment to making a positive impact on people's lives.

Chapter 8

Vision for the Future

Keir Starmer's vision for the future outlines his hopes and plans for making life better for everyone. This chapter explores his goals for creating jobs, improving healthcare, and ensuring fair opportunities for all. Understanding Keir's vision helps us see how he wants to build a society where everyone has a chance to succeed and where fairness and compassion are at the heart of policymaking. It's about looking forward to a brighter future where challenges are met with unity and determination.

8.1 Starmer's vision for the Labour Party

Keir Starmer's vision for the Labour Party focuses on unity, fairness, and practical solutions to improve people's lives. He believes in rebuilding the party as a strong and inclusive force that represents the diverse interests of all communities across the UK.

Firstly, Keir aims to unite the Labour Party by bridging internal divides and promoting a sense of common purpose. He emphasises the importance of solidarity among party members and values diversity of opinion within the party. By fostering unity, he believes Labour can present a cohesive front and effectively challenge the government on behalf of the people.

Fairness is a cornerstone of Keir's vision. He advocates for policies that reduce inequality and create opportunities for everyone to thrive. This includes initiatives to support working families, improve public services like healthcare and education, and ensure fair wages and job security. Keir believes in a society where everyone has a fair chance to succeed, regardless of their background or circumstances.

Keir's vision for the Labour Party includes a commitment to practical and evidence-based policymaking. He emphasises the importance of listening to experts, consulting with communities, and developing policies that are grounded in real-world needs and experiences. Keir aims to present Labour as a credible alternative government by offering pragmatic solutions to complex challenges such as climate change, economic recovery, and social justice.

Keir prioritises honesty and transparency in his leadership approach. He believes in holding the government accountable for its actions and promises, while also being open about Labour's own plans and commitments to the public. This transparency is essential for rebuilding trust with voters and demonstrating Labour's reliability as a political party.

Keir Starmer's vision for the Labour Party revolves around unity, fairness, practicality, and transparency. He seeks to lead Labour towards becoming a party that stands for social justice, economic opportunity, and a better future for all Britons. His vision aims to resonate with a broad spectrum of voters and rebuild Labour's reputation as a party capable of governing responsibly and effectively.

8.2 Policy priorities and long-term goals

Keir Starmer's policy priorities and long-term goals outline his plans to address key issues facing the UK, focusing on improving people's lives and building a fairer society for all.

One of Keir's main policy priorities is to strengthen the economy and create more jobs. He believes in investing in infrastructure projects, such as building new homes and improving public transport, to stimulate economic growth and provide employment opportunities. Keir aims to support small businesses and industries that have been hit hard by economic challenges, ensuring they have the resources they need to recover and thrive.

Education is another critical area for Keir. He prioritises increasing funding for schools and ensuring that every child has access to high-quality education. This includes reducing class sizes, improving teacher training, and investing in school facilities. Keir is committed to addressing educational inequalities and providing support for students from disadvantaged backgrounds to succeed academically.

Healthcare is a top priority for Keir, who advocates for strengthening the National Health Service (NHS). He aims to increase funding for healthcare services, reduce waiting times for treatments, and improve access to mental health support. Keir also supports measures to address public health challenges, such as obesity and smoking, to promote healthier lifestyles across the UK.

In terms of social justice, Keir is dedicated to tackling inequality and discrimination in all its forms. He supports policies to promote equal pay, protect workers' rights, and advance LGBTQ+ rights. Keir believes in fostering a society where everyone is treated with dignity and respect, regardless of their race, gender, or sexual orientation.

Climate change is another pressing issue for Keir, who emphasises the importance of taking decisive action to protect the environment. He supports transitioning to renewable energy sources, reducing carbon emissions, and investing in green technologies. Keir aims to position the

UK as a global leader in the fight against climate change, creating green jobs and promoting sustainable development practices.

Long-term, Keir's goals include building a more united and cohesive society where everyone has opportunities to succeed and thrive. He envisions a future where social mobility is enhanced, communities are empowered, and the benefits of economic growth are shared more equitably. Keir also aims to strengthen the UK's international relationships and play a constructive role in global issues such as human rights, international development, and peacekeeping.

Keir Starmer's policy priorities and long-term goals revolve around strengthening the economy, improving education and healthcare, promoting social justice, tackling climate change, and building a more united society. His vision for the UK is grounded in fairness, opportunity, and sustainability, aiming to address current challenges while laying the foundation for a brighter future for all Britons.

8.3 Potential impact on British politics

Keir Starmer could greatly influence British politics through his leadership style and key priorities. His focus on uniting the Labour Party may strengthen its position. By bringing together different groups and fostering a sense of shared purpose, he aims to present a strong alternative to the current government. This unity could improve Labour's chances in future elections and enhance its ability to challenge the government effectively.

Keir's emphasis on fairness and social justice resonates with many voters concerned about inequality and government policies' impact on daily life. His plans to improve education, healthcare, and job opportunities could appeal broadly, especially to those feeling neglected or disadvantaged under current policies.

Keir's commitment to openness and honesty in leadership could help rebuild trust in politics. By being transparent about Labour's plans and holding the government accountable for its actions, he aims to restore faith in how decisions are made and ensure they benefit the public.

Additionally, Keir's stance on climate change and the environment positions Labour as a leader in sustainability. His support for renewable energy and efforts to cut carbon emissions could attract voters concerned about the planet's future and eager for stronger environmental action.

Keir Starmer's potential to impact British politics lies in his ability to unite his party, appeal broadly with his fairness and justice agenda, restore trust in leadership, and lead on critical issues like climate change. His leadership style and vision for a fairer, greener society have the potential to shape the future of British politics significantly.

Chapter 9

Legacy and Critique

Keir Starmer's journey in politics and law has left a lasting mark, and this chapter looks at how his work will be remembered. We'll explore the significant changes he brought about, the lives he impacted, and the lasting influence he hopes to have on British society. Additionally, we'll discuss the criticisms and challenges he faced along the way, providing a balanced view of his legacy. This chapter aims to give a complete picture of his contributions and the debates they sparked.

9.1 Achievements, Contributions, Criticisms, and Controversies

Keir Starmer's career is filled with notable successes and contributions, but it also includes its fair share of criticisms and controversies. Keir Starmer has accomplished a lot throughout his career. As Director of Public Prosecutions (DPP), he handled some of the UK's most famous cases. One of his major achievements was leading the prosecution of the killers of Damilola Taylor, a young boy whose death shocked the nation. Keir's determination and thoroughness helped secure justice for Damilola's family.

Another significant case was the prosecution of Levi Bellfield, a serial killer responsible for the deaths of several young women. This case was complex and difficult, but Keir's leadership ensured that Bellfield was convicted, providing closure for the victims' families.

Keir also worked on the case of Rachel Nickell, a young mother murdered on Wimbledon Common. After years of failed attempts and setbacks, Keir's team finally secured a conviction, showcasing his persistence and dedication to justice.

In politics, Keir has made important contributions. As an MP, he quickly became known for his work on human rights and justice. He has been a strong advocate for equality and fairness, pushing for policies to support the most vulnerable people in society. His efforts to improve workers' rights and ensure better working conditions are notable, as is his commitment to addressing climate change through sustainable policies.

Despite his many achievements, Keir Starmer has faced his share of criticisms and controversies. As DPP, some people felt that he was too cautious in deciding whether to prosecute certain cases, leading to frustration among those seeking justice. For example, his decision not to prosecute the police officers involved in the death of Ian Tomlinson, a newspaper seller who died during the 2009 G20 protests, led to significant public outcry and debate.

In his political career, Keir's stance on Brexit was a source of criticism from both sides. As a strong advocate for a second referendum, he faced backlash from Leave supporters who believed he was undermining the decision to leave the EU. Meanwhile, some Remain supporters felt he didn't do enough to stop Brexit, leaving him caught in the middle of a highly divisive issue.

Keir's leadership of the Labour Party has also been under scrutiny. Some party members believe he hasn't done enough to unite the party or present a clear alternative to the Conservative government. His handling of internal disputes and disciplinary issues, especially related to accusations of antisemitism, has also been controversial. Critics argue that he has struggled to balance different factions within the party and address long-standing issues effectively.

Keir Starmer's career involves balancing his desire to bring about positive change with the challenges of navigating complex political and legal landscapes. His commitment to justice and fairness is clear, but so are the difficulties he faced in trying to implement his vision. The criticisms and controversies he encounters highlight the complexities of leadership and the inevitable conflicts that arise when trying to meet the needs of a diverse and divided audience.

Keir's achievements, especially in law and order, show his capability and dedication. However, his political journey underscores the tough realities of public service, where decisions are constantly scrutinised and often met with mixed reactions. His handling of Brexit and internal Labour Party issues reflects the broader struggles of finding common ground in a polarised society.

As Keir Starmer continues his leadership, it remains to be seen how he will navigate these challenges and build on his achievements. His ability to address criticisms, unify his party, and clearly articulate his vision for the future will be crucial. The legacy he leaves behind will depend not only on his successes but also on how he learns from and responds to the controversies and criticisms he faces.

Keir Starmer's journey shows his resilience and dedication to public service. His contributions have made a significant impact, but his career also highlights the inherent difficulties and controversies that come with leadership. How he balances these elements will shape his lasting legacy in British politics and law.

9.2 Views and Insights from Others

Keir Starmer's career has generated a variety of opinions from colleagues, political analysts, and the public. Some see him as a strong and principled leader, while others have reservations.

Many people in the Labour Party admire Keir Starmer for his intelligence and dedication. They believe he is capable of leading the party through tough times. His background as a lawyer and his role as Director of Public Prosecutions show that he can handle complex issues and make difficult decisions. Colleagues often praise his calm nature and ability to stay focused under pressure. They feel that his professional experience adds seriousness and credibility to his leadership.

Political analysts have mixed opinions on Starmer. Some think his focus on unity and fairness is exactly what the Labour Party needs. They appreciate his efforts to bring different groups within the party together and present a clear alternative to the current government. These analysts believe that his emphasis on social justice and equality resonates with many voters, especially those who feel left behind by other leaders.

However, not all analysts are convinced by Starmer's approach. Some criticise him for being too cautious and not taking bold enough steps to stand out from his predecessors or the Conservative government. They argue that he needs to be more dynamic and assertive to gain the support of the broader public. Critics feel that while his policies are well-meaning, they sometimes lack the clarity and boldness needed to inspire confidence and drive significant change.

Public opinion on Keir Starmer is also divided. Many people appreciate his commitment to justice and fairness. They see him as a principled leader who genuinely cares about making society more equal. His efforts to improve education, healthcare, and workers' rights are seen as positive steps toward creating a fairer society. Supporters believe that his background in law gives him a strong foundation for understanding and addressing the challenges facing the country.

On the other hand, some members of the public feel that Starmer has not done enough to distinguish himself from previous Labour leaders. They worry that his cautious approach might prevent him from making the bold changes needed to tackle the UK's biggest issues. Some people also feel that he has not effectively communicated his vision for the country, leaving them unsure about what he stands for and how he plans to achieve his goals.

Insights from people who have worked closely with Starmer provide additional depth to these views. Former colleagues from his time as Director of Public Prosecutions describe him as meticulous and dedicated. They recall his commitment to ensuring that justice was served and his willingness to take on challenging cases. These colleagues often speak of his integrity and determination to do what is right, even when it is difficult.

Politicians who have interacted with Starmer in Parliament also have varied opinions. Some respect his legal expertise and his calm, measured approach to debates and discussions. They believe that his focus on facts and evidence helps to elevate the quality of political discussions.

However, others feel that he sometimes comes across as too reserved or cautious, which can make it difficult for him to connect with voters on a personal level.

Views and insights on Keir Starmer show a complex picture. His intelligence, dedication, and commitment to justice are widely acknowledged and appreciated. Many see him as a principled leader capable of guiding the Labour Party through difficult times. However, there are also concerns about his cautious approach and whether he can inspire the bold changes needed to address the UK's issues. As Starmer continues his leadership journey, the diverse perspectives on his work and impact will shape his legacy and influence his ability to achieve his goals.

9.3 Starmer's own reflections and Lessons from his career

Keir Starmer has had a long and varied career, learning many important lessons along the way. When he looks back on his journey, he often talks about the values that have guided him and the insights he has gained from his experiences.

One key lesson for Starmer is the importance of perseverance. Throughout his career, he has faced many challenges and setbacks. Whether it was handling tough legal cases as Director of Public Prosecutions or dealing with conflicts within the Labour Party, Starmer learned that persistence is crucial. He believes that staying committed to one's goals, even when things get difficult, is essential for making real change.

Starmer also highlights the value of integrity. In his legal career, he often had to make tough decisions that involved balancing different interests and navigating ethical issues. He has always tried to stay true to his principles, believing that honesty and transparency are vital for maintaining public trust. This commitment to integrity has shaped how he leads and makes decisions in politics as well.

Another important lesson for Starmer has been the power of collaboration.

Throughout his career, he has worked with many different people, from fellow lawyers to political colleagues and community leaders. He has seen how bringing different perspectives together can help solve problems. Starmer believes that listening to others and working as a team are essential for creating effective solutions and making progress.

Starmer often reflects on the importance of empathy. He has spent much of his career advocating for justice and fairness, believing that understanding and addressing the needs of the most vulnerable in society is a key duty of leadership. Whether it's fighting for better workers' rights or pushing for policies to tackle inequality, Starmer's commitment to empathy has guided his work.

He also recognizes the value of learning from mistakes. Starmer admits that he hasn't always gotten everything right, but he believes that each mistake is a chance to learn and improve. This humility and willingness to grow have helped him handle the complexities of his roles and adapt to new challenges.

Starmer emphasises the importance of vision. He believes that leaders need to have a clear and compelling vision for the future, and they must be able to communicate this vision effectively. Throughout his career, he has worked to share his ideas for a fairer, more just society, and he continues to strive toward these goals.

Keir Starmer's reflections on his career highlight the lessons he has learned about perseverance, integrity, collaboration, empathy, learning from mistakes, and the importance of vision. These insights have shaped how he leads and continue to guide him as he works to make a positive impact on British politics and society.

Conclusion

Keir Starmer's journey has been long and eventful, marked by significant achievements and challenges. His career began in law, where he made a name for himself as a dedicated and principled lawyer. As Director of Public Prosecutions, he handled some of the UK's most high-profile cases, demonstrating his commitment to justice and fairness. These experiences laid a strong foundation for his later political career.

When Starmer transitioned to politics, he brought with him the same dedication and principles that defined his legal work. As an MP, he quickly became known for his focus on social justice and equality. His work on human rights and workers' rights showed his deep commitment to making society fairer for everyone. His calm and focused approach earned him respect from many colleagues and analysts.

As leader of the Labour Party, Starmer faced the enormous challenge of uniting a divided party and presenting a clear alternative to the Conservative government. His efforts to bring different factions together and his focus on evidence-based policies have been notable. However, he has also faced criticism for being too cautious and not bold enough in his approach. Balancing these different demands has been a complex task.

Looking to the future, Keir Starmer has a lot of potential. His intelligence, dedication, and commitment to justice are clear strengths. If he can effectively communicate his vision and take bold steps to address the UK's pressing issues, he has the potential to make a significant impact. His focus on social justice, equality, and fairness aligns with the values of many voters, and his professional background gives him a strong foundation to address the country's challenges.

However, the road ahead will not be easy. Starmer will need to navigate the complexities of modern politics, address internal party conflicts, and respond to criticisms of his leadership style. He will also need to connect more effectively with voters, showing them not just his plans but also his passion and vision for a better future. This means being more dynamic and assertive in his approach, while still staying true to his principles of integrity and fairness.

In conclusion, Keir Starmer's journey so far has been marked by dedication and a strong commitment to justice and fairness. His career in law and politics has shown his ability to handle complex issues and make tough decisions. While he faces significant challenges as the leader of the Labour Party, his potential to make a positive impact on British politics is clear. By staying true to his principles and taking bold steps to address the country's issues, he can work towards creating a fairer, more just society.

Starmer's story is one of perseverance and integrity. His reflections on his career highlight the lessons he has learned and the values that guide him. As he continues his leadership journey, these principles will be crucial in shaping his legacy and influence. The future holds many uncertainties, but with his focus on social justice and equality, Keir Starmer has the potential to leave a lasting mark on British politics. His journey is far from over, and the next steps he takes will be crucial in defining his impact and legacy.